CLASS

Charles Evered

BROADWAY PLAY PUBLISHING INC
New York
www.broadwayplaypublishing.com
info@broadwayplaypublishing.com

CLASS

© Copyright 2010, 2011, 2016 by Charles Evered

Cover graphic: Jacqueline Gaul
Cover photo by Jill Mamey

I S B N: 978-0-88145-477-2

First printing: November 2010
Second printing: November 2011
Third printing, revised: January 2016

Book design: Marie Donovan
Page make-up: Adobe Indesign
Typeface: Palatino
Printed and bound in the U S A

CLASS premiered at Cape May Stage, Cape May, NJ, on 15 May 2010. The cast and creative contributors were:

SARAH.. Heather Matarazzo
ELLIOT..Thaao Penghlis

Director.. Roy B Steinberg
Stage manager....................................Matthew Kurtis Lutz
Scenic design...Sarah Lambert
Costumes.. Robert J Martin
Sound ....Dennis Zaicevs
Lighting...Jeffrey Salzberg
Playwright's assistant ....Melissa Harkness

CLASS was subsequently produced in 2015 at Falcon Theatre in Burbank, California. The cast and creative contributors were:

SARAH..Callie Schuttera
ELLIOT.. Gildart Jackson

Director..Dimitri Toscas
Set .... Francois-Pierre Couture
Costumes.. Terri A Lewis
Lighting..Nick McCord

Special thanks to those who have helped in the development of the play, including: Eric Barr, Roger Rees, Bebe Neuwirth, Paul Jacques, Patrick Brien, Rob Jacklosky, the 3 Theater Group, Joe Brancato, Garry Marshall, and Kathleen Marshall LaGambina.

CHARACTERS & SETTING

SARAH, *early 20s*
ELLIOT, *middle age*

The play takes place in an acting studio in New York City.

The time is the present.

Scene One

(Lights up as ELLIOT *walks into the studio. There's a worn hard wood floor, and some windows overlooking the street, which is only a floor or two down. There are scattered chairs, a riser and assorted rehearsal props lying about.)*

*(*ELLIOT *addresses the audience as though they were his students.)*

ELLIOT: Oh, look at you all. Warms the cockles doesn't it? A new fresh faced batch of acting students. Positively bright eyed and bushytailed. Ironic though, because even though you possessed enough of something to make it into this class, the truth is—most of you will never make it. The overwhelming majority of you will never make a living as an actor, the harsh reality being—you will probably spend thousands of dollars you don't actually have, in pursuit of a dream that will remain elusive. You will take out loans, you will borrow from friends, sleep on couches into your thirties and forties, —your adolescence will be extended until it's embarrassing to everyone around you, holidays will become hell for you, as you sit around the family dinner table and your parents quiz your more successful siblings, only to eventually settle upon you—and after an interminably awkward pause, you will regale them with stories of the unpaid Equity showcase you just appeared in, in which you earned subway fare and free bagels—and were directed by a creepy trust fund idiot who made you dress up like a carrot shaped dwarf. Yes, welcome to your future ladies and gentlemen. The upside? Well, if things work out, you can perhaps change the world—or at least your little corner of it. You will know the sublime sensation of practicing an art that is more than honorable—and before you die, you may very well touch the hearts of tens, hundreds, thousands, who knows—maybe even millions of people you never met before, and in doing so, perhaps change their lives as well. But, as I've already mentioned—that probably won't be happening to anyone in this room. Just so we're clear. Now, lets get started, shall we?

(Lights bump to black.)

Scene Two

(Later that day)

(ELLIOT is alone in the studio, about to head out. A beautiful young woman [SARAH] walks in. She's wearing dark glasses and a baseball cap pulled low over her forehead.)

SARAH: I think I'm probably—yeah, I think I'm probably lost.

ELLIOT: Who are you looking for?

SARAH: Elliot.

ELLIOT: I'm Elliot.

SARAH: Oh well—wow! Well, great, I guess I'm not lost.

ELLIOT: If only it were that easy.

SARAH: Sorry?

ELLIOT: If only finding what we were looking for meant we still weren't lost.

SARAH: Oh, yeah—wow. Wow, that is like—wow, that is—

ELLIOT: How can I help you?

SARAH: I want to take a class.

ELLIOT: You're too late. I start sessions at the beginning of each month.

SARAH: Oh, well, can I—

ELLIOT: —no.

SARAH: —no, I mean—

ELLIOT: —it doesn't matter what you mean. I start the sessions at the beginning of each month.

SARAH: Well I just assumed—

ELLIOT: —well, that's just the problem, isn't it?

SARAH: Wow, you're kind of like, mean.

ELLIOT: Actually, I'm kind of "like" reasonable.

SARAH: Oh my God, are you like—making fun of me?

ELLIOT: Oh my God, I think I "like" —totally am.

SARAH: I'm not stupid, you know. I just didn't think you'd be such an uptight dude.

ELLIOT: Did you just call me a "dude"?

SARAH: I just want to take a class.

ELLIOT: I've already told you when classes start.

SARAH: Then I'll study privately, with you.

ELLIOT: Private study is by invitation only.

SARAH: Then invite me.

ELLIOT: You have to audition to get invited.

SARAH: Audition?

ELLIOT: That's right. How did you find me anyway?

SARAH: Roger.

ELLIOT: Roger who?

SARAH: My agent.

ELLIOT: What is his last name?

SARAH: Bilotti.

ELLIOT: Bilotti? How did he know me?

SARAH: He said he took a class with you.

ELLIOT: More than one Roger has.

SARAH: He said you're the best.

ELLIOT: A lot of people say that. Anyhoo, it's been positively, I don't know—something—talking to you, but alas I'm late for an appointment. So, if you'll excuse me— (*He starts to walk past her.*)

SARAH: I hope you don't mind my saying, but you have been a real disappointment.

(ELLIOT *stops.*)

ELLIOT: Excuse me?

SARAH: I guess I just had an image, you know, —of what a "legit" type New York acting teacher would be like.

ELLIOT: Gee whiz, and I didn't live up to your expectations?

SARAH: To be honest, no, you haven't.

ELLIOT: Hmm. Well, I'm sorry about that. I could imagine it's going to take me some time to recover from my own disappointment—with myself—at having disappointed you—whomever you are. Before I go however, would you mind if I gave you just a bit of unsolicited advice?

SARAH: Whatever.

ELLIOT: Change everything about yourself. Your attitude, your weak posture, your inflated self regard, and as for your breathing, more diaphragmatic

please—not through your teeth so much. Also, look
people in the eyes, —which means don't be so rude
as to leave sunglasses on when you're still inside. As
for filling out your personal character, perhaps you
might consider volunteering—maybe join the Peace
Corp or something. Oh, and if you've had them done,
which I'm assuming you have—have your breasts
made smaller, more proportional to your body. If you
haven't had them done, congratulations to you and
do more sit ups. Wear less makeup and have enough
respect for people to properly introduce yourself when
you meet them. And last but not least, turn off the
lights when you leave. Goodnight.

(ELLIOT *puts on his cap, smiles, turns and walks out the
door. The* WOMAN *stands frozen as the lights fade to black.)*

Scene Three

(The next day)

(As the lights come up, we see SARAH *lying on her back, in
the middle of the floor. She's still wearing her baseball hat
and dark glasses. As she lies perfectly still, facing up toward
the ceiling, she recites the word "space," deliberately, to
herself. After she says it about three times, we see* ELLIOT
*walk in. He takes note of her. She doesn't notice him
however, almost as though she were in a trance, and she
continues reciting "space." He hangs up his coat. Finally,
she stops reciting "space" and calmly begins talking to him
while she remains on the floor.)*

SARAH: Surprised to see me?

ELLIOT: I must admit I am.

(WOMAN *gets up, taking off her dark glasses for the first
time.)*

SARAH: Sarah by the way.

ELLIOT: That's terrific. And you—unless I'm mistaken, are trespassing in my "space".

SARAH: I couldn't wait outside.

ELLIOT: Was I unclear yesterday?

SARAH: No, you were very clear.

ELLIOT: Then what are you doing in my— "space"?

SARAH: Please don't make fun of my process.

ELLIOT: Your what?

SARAH: That's what I do. That's what I do to prepare. I really thought you'd be more open-minded.

ELLIOT: Let me ask you: what twenty dollar an hour audit encouraging hack convinced you that lying on a dusty floor and reciting one word over and over again had anything to do whatsoever with preparing yourself as an actor?

SARAH: Well, if you must know—

ELLIOT: —and why do you look so familiar to me?

SARAH: I have one of those faces.

ELLIOT: No, but it's like I've seen it before.

SARAH: You saw it yesterday.

ELLIOT: No, I mean before that.

SARAH: I get that a lot.

(ELLIOT *gravitates toward a window, looks down.*)

ELLIOT: Did you notice that commotion out front?

SARAH: I did.

ELLIOT: I've never seen so many photographers in my life.

SARAH: Listen, you have to take me on. I've done my homework on you, ya know. Or, well, okay, I had someone else do it for me, but I did in the end, read all the condensed versions of the notes they made up for me about you—and I'm convinced you're the only person who could help me.

ELLIOT: Someone makes up "condensed versions" of notes for you? Aren't "notes" by their very nature "condensed"? And what was that? You've done your "homework" on me?

SARAH: Of course I did. Do you think I'd make a fool out of myself two days in a row if I didn't like, sorry about the "like", —if I didn't know this was right? That this was what I needed? All I want, more than anything in the whole world is to be a *real* actor.

ELLIOT: Not good enough.

SARAH: What?

ELLIOT: Not good enough. Wanting has nothing to do with it.

SARAH: I'm in a position to pay you by the way—much more, I'm sure, than you're usually paid.

ELLIOT: Oh, really? Well, then in that case get out.

SARAH: Wait, what? Did you just hear what I said?

ELLIOT: I could ask the same of you.

SARAH: Well, did I offend you, or—

ELLIOT: —why would I be offended by your making the assumption I could be bought off like a cheap whore?

SARAH: Well, that's not how I meant it.

ELLIOT: Isn't it?

SARAH: I'm just saying, I mean—look at this place.

ELLIOT: Excuse me?

SARAH: I'm just saying. I'm not making any judgments.

ELLIOT: And how much theatre experience do you have exactly?

SARAH: Well you mean, like what—like, actually being on stage and stuff?

ELLIOT: Yes, not counting elementary school.

SARAH: Well, —

ELLIOT: —or high school.

SARAH: Oh. Then, uhm—

ELLIOT: Okay, moving on from those minor stumbling blocks—tell me, succinctly and with clarity— Why it is—exactly, you want to be an actor.

SARAH: Well, because—I uhm—

ELLIOT: Go on.

SARAH: Well— (*She can't formulate anything, just looks back at him.*)

ELLIOT: Right, so just to sum this up. You have no practical theatrical experience whatsoever —outside of elementary and high school and you have no idea why it is you want to be an actor. Or, even if you do have an idea, you are wholly incapable of articulating it in any manner whatsoever. Do I have that right so far?

SARAH: I'm sorry, Elliot, I didn't mean to waste your—

(SARAH *leaves.* ELLIOT *stands frozen himself, as an air of regret hangs about him as slowly, she appears back at the door.*)

SARAH: The story.

ELLIOT: Say again?

SARAH: Why I want to act. It's the story. It's not my father, honestly, I know that's what most people think with actresses—that we all have fathers that ignore us and so—well, my father is really quite wonderful, and my mother is a gas, really. I'm actually very lucky that way. No, for me, it was the kitchen table. All of us—I come from a big family, and I used to do these little characters, voices, nothing elaborate, but it was the way I communicated with everyone. We didn't talk, you know, *really* talk to one another, so I would try to make the rest of my family laugh, and I would invent these interwoven little stories—play these odd little characters: *(Doing the accents)* the Slovakian man with little carrots in his nose, the old English lady with a beard of pudding on her chin, just these stupid characters and hammy little voices and seeing how it made them laugh or smile—for even a little while. Or maybe even just to forget things. But mostly it was to make them smile.

ELLIOT: Smile at you, you mean?

SARAH: No, I know that's what you're thinking, but it wasn't that they were smiling at me—it was that they were smiling.

(SARAH starts out. ELLIOT calls out:)

ELLIOT: Thursdays.

(SARAH stops.)

SARAH: What?

ELLIOT: Thursdays. I might have some time on Thursdays, between four and five.

SARAH: Well, —oh my gosh, well—well, that would be—

ELLIOT: And don't ever ever ever ever *ever* be late.

SARAH: I won't be.

ELLIOT: And don't say the "space" thing out loud again. It makes you sound—well—

SARAH: I won't. Thank you.

(SARAH *smiles, puts on her dark glasses, turns and leaves as the lights fade to black.*)

Scene Four

(*The following Thursday*)

(*As the lights come up, we see* SARAH *lying in the middle of the floor again, but silently.* ELLIOT *walks in.*)

SARAH: Don't worry, I'm not going to say that word. Not even in my head.

ELLIOT: I can't tell you how relieved I am to hear that.

(SARAH *gets up, looks over at* ELLIOT.)

SARAH: Okay, so how do you want to get started?

ELLIOT: I have a little ritual I do at the beginning of each class, and I don't see any point in conducting this one any differently.

SARAH: Great, I love rituals, what is it?

(ELLIOT *walks over to a prop hat, turns to* SARAH *with it.*)

ELLIOT: It's simple. I pass a hat around, and students write down a question—anything at all, on a slip of paper. Anonymously of course, and I answer it. I find it a great way to clear the air as it were.

SARAH: I am however—the only student in this class.

ELLIOT: Your point?

SARAH: Well it kind of negates the "anonymity" aspect of it, wouldn't you say?

ELLIOT: A ritual *is* a ritual.

SARAH: Fine. (*She goes over to her purse, takes out a little slip of paper and a pen, writes on it, then, walks back over to* ELLIOT *and drops the piece of paper in the hat.*) Let 'er rip.

(ELLIOT *starts to shake the hat.*)

SARAH: What are you doing?

ELLIOT: Shaking. Only fair.

(SARAH *rolls her eyes*)

ELLIOT: All right, all right. (*He looks down at the hat.*)
Oh look, here's one! (*He pulls the piece of paper out of the hat, opens it and reads aloud.*) "Are you always such an asshole?" (*He looks up, as though scanning an imaginary audience.*) To whomever wrote this scurrilous little note. "Yes, in fact I am."

SARAH: I feel the air clearing already, don't you?

ELLIOT: You're forgetting to breathe by the way.

SARAH: What?

ELLIOT: You're not breathing. You are breathing enough to stay alive, but otherwise, you're hardly breathing at all.

SARAH: I thought I was breathing just fine.

ELLIOT: You weren't, come on now—follow me:
Breathe! Come on! Breathe!

(SARAH *takes a deep breath.*)

ELLIOT: That's pathetic. Really open up, come on, breathe!

(SARAH *takes an even deeper breath.*)

ELLIOT: Now *that* is more like it!

SARAH: Wow, that did kind of relax me. So what do we do now? You want me to do a monologue, what?

ELLIOT: Actually, I'd like to start by telling you what an interesting morning I had.

SARAH: Oh, okay.

ELLIOT: Usual start of the day for me. Up at the crack of eleven, brew myself a cup of coffee—counting on the caffeine kicking in just about the same time self-loathing would—which is a good thing for me—because I find the effect of the caffeine and the self-loathing tend to cancel each other out. Though on this particular morning I found myself out of coffee altogether.

SARAH: Yipes.

ELLIOT: Yes, "yipes". So I pulled on my shoes and out I sprang, thinking perhaps if I could get my caffeine fast enough, maybe, just maybe—I could outrun the self-loathing.

SARAH: Well did you?

ELLIOT: Not quite I'm afraid. As it turns out, just as I was about to cross Sixth Avenue, the "Walk" sign changed and I skidded to a halt—just before a long, slow bus pulled out in front of me.

SARAH: Okay.

ELLIOT: Right. And on the side of that bus was a huge, brightly colored—movie poster.

SARAH: Well, that's not unusual.

ELLIOT: No, it isn't. What is unusual however, is that smack dab in the middle of that huge poster, was a huge face. A very pretty, I must say, but very familiar face.

SARAH: Ah ha.

ELLIOT: Right, and so there I was. Staring face to face with this—face. And then it hit me.

SARAH: The bus?

ELLIOT: I'm afraid not. No, it occurred to me where I had seen this face before.

SARAH: And where was that?

ELLIOT: Everywhere. *(Pause)* You might have at least mentioned—in passing anyway, that you are what the world refers to as a "movie star".

SARAH: I was going to say something, but I was shocked, —honestly, but not in an egotistical way—that you didn't recognize me. I mean I wasn't purposefully avoiding telling you. I was just so thrilled you didn't seem to know.

(ELLIOT goes to window, looks down.)

ELLIOT: And those idiots with the cameras down there?

SARAH: Comes with the territory I'm afraid.

ELLIOT: "Comes with the territory?" What are they waiting for?

SARAH: They're waiting for me to come out.

ELLIOT: And do what?

SARAH: Walk to my car.

ELLIOT: Wait, you got a parking space in Midtown?

SARAH: No. I have a car. You know, with a driver— waiting for me.

ELLIOT: "Waiting" for you? And what will they do when you go out there?

SARAH: The same thing they did when I walked in— they'll take pictures of me—yell things at me, hopefully embarrass or anger me. Try to get me to say things or do things that will make the pictures worth more money. This is all stupid, I know.

ELLIOT: —and what was that thing you were holding?

SARAH: Where?

ELLIOT: On the movie poster, on the bus. There was something in your hand. Held up, just to the left of your pouty candy red lips. What was it, a gun?

SARAH: No, it's a skorcon cyberblaster.

ELLIOT: A what?

SARAH: It's sort of like a gun—a space gun that my character uses in the movie. It's a space movie, but a kind of sexy action one.

ELLIOT: A skorcon cyberblaster.

SARAH: Do you see now? Do you see now, why I didn't want to—

ELLIOT: —give me an example of some of the dialogue you have in that movie.

SARAH: That's not the only movie I've made by the way. I've made quite a few, you know, and some of them are like, not quite as bad as that one. Sorry about the "like."

ELLIOT: Okay, okay, I just want to hear some of what you have to say in the movie.

SARAH: But why?

ELLIOT: Because I asked!

SARAH: Alright! Okay, my character is Doomnessa, and she's—

ELLIOT: Wait, what's her name?

SARAH: Doomnessa. She's from the fictional planet Noomjohn.

ELLIOT: I see, and Doomnessa says what?

SARAH: Well, at one point—in about the middle of the movie, Doomnessa is running through the Panthorian ecoplex, kind of like a virtual spacey kind of hall of mirrors, and she's trying to get away from the Glitterods, who—

ELLIOT: …do spare me the "plot". Just give me an example of some of her dialogue.

SARAH: Alright, fine: *(Readies herself, then)* "Noomjohnians hear me! Hurt the Glitterods not, for they too are worthy of our compassion. They are not human, perhaps, but they are people just the same."

(SARAH looks over at ELLIOT, who is fairly horrified.)

SARAH: What? It's a message of inclusion.

ELLIOT: Right, thank you for that clarification. It was so subtle and buried so organically in the text, I hadn't had a chance to process it.

SARAH: This isn't very fair, you know. I mean it's easy to make fun of something like that.

ELLIOT: Yes, and why do you think that is?

SARAH: —oh right, and everything you "legit" theatre types do is sooo pristine.

ELLIOT: Meaning?

SARAH: I'm just saying, —there's all kinds of crap. The movie industry doesn't have a monopoly on it, that's all.

ELLIOT: Have you ever heard of a writer by the name of William Shakespeare?

SARAH: Screw you, Elliot.

ELLIOT: Oh, would you hold on one second? I just have to— *(He wanders out the door and into the hall. We hear him from the hallway:)* Sorry, I know it's out here somewhere.

SARAH: What are you looking for?

ELLIOT: *(From the hall)* Your sense of humor. *(He comes back in)* I could have sworn I saw it near the elevator.

SARAH: Yes, I've read Shakespeare.

ELLIOT: Well then you realize with no doubt whatsoever—that if the Bard of Avon had access to that—what was it—the "scorecard cybo—"

SARAH: Skorcon cyberblaster.

ELLIOT: Right, the skorcon cyberblaster—he would have used it in a heartbeat.

SARAH: Now you're being all cheeky.

ELLIOT: Oh, on the contrary. CUT TO: Macduff, going all whoopass on Macbeth—skorcon cyberblaster marks all up and down MacBeth's backside. Don't even get me started on what the body count in Titus would have been. No, are you kidding me? Old Will wasn't shy about spicing up the joint. Let me tell ya. First things first, the man knew how to get butts in seats.

SARAH: What is it you're trying to tell me?

ELLIOT: Lighten up! Simple as that. "Doomnessa" —did you have fun with her?

SARAH: I did actually.

ELLIOT: Did you show up to the set on time?

SARAH: Usually.

ELLIOT: "Usually"?

SARAH: I'm working on that.

ELLIOT: Were you respectful to your fellow actors? Did you listen? Did you give them something to work with?

SARAH: I'd like to think I did.

ELLIOT: Then take the Mount Rushmore sized chip off your shoulder, pocket the half a mil or whatever it was they paid you to play dress up and count your lucky stars.

SARAH: "Half a mil"? (She starts to laugh.)

ELLIOT: What?

SARAH: "Half a million?" Do you mean in "dollars" or—?

ELLIOT: What? What's so funny?

(SARAH *laughs harder.*)

ELLIOT: What? Why are you laughing?

SARAH: You're just—you're just so sweet.

ELLIOT: "Sweet"? You couldn't be more patronizing. Why, what did they pay you then?

SARAH: Come on, it doesn't matter.

ELLIOT: No, I'd like to know. I'm such a dinosaur, I want to know what a dinosaur I am. How much?

SARAH: I don't know, seven? Seven and a half? Plus a percentage of the gross. But, you know, Elliot, after everybody takes their cut, lawyers, publicists, agents, Uncle Sam—

ELLIOT: Wait, they paid you seven million dollars to play some space trollop running around with a cyber basket or whatever it is?

SARAH: Cyberblaster.

ELLIOT: Whatever! That is obscene. That is—

SARAH: —oh, look who's lost his sense of humor now.

ELLIOT: Well that's ridiculous.

SARAH: It isn't a grant, Elliot. It's not like its coming out of your pocket.

ELLIOT: But that is—no. No, that is just—no, that is just, no—that is just disgusting. That is just—no, that is just—

SARAH: —see, I knew you were a snob.

ELLIOT: I am not, I just have a sense of proportion. And when that sense is violated I react.

SARAH: What is so out of proportion?

ELLIOT: Your salary.

SARAH: Is it really? what would you have me do, take less? To save who money? Save those poor, starving suits at the studio some much needed cabbage? I think not. It's all relative Elliot, you know that. All it is is money.

ELLIOT: Did I happen to mention my rates have gone up?

SARAH: Oh, really? And when did that happen?

ELLIOT: Just about forty seconds ago in fact.

SARAH: Is that right?

ELLIOT: Oh, yes, all of it being "relative" and all.

SARAH: Can we not work today? I'm not feeling well I'm afraid.

ELLIOT: Oh, don't say that—you know what happens to characters who say that.

SARAH: What do you mean?

ELLIOT: Well, when a character says he or she isn't "feeling well." Not good news for him or her usually.

SARAH: I didn't realize.

ELLIOT: Indeed. Sort of a universal dramatic red flag.

SARAH: Is that right? *(She just looks at him.)*

ELLIOT: Anyway, let me get you some water.

SARAH: No, I'm alright, I'm just tired. I could use a cup of coffee though. What do you say I call my driver and he can bring some up for us.

ELLIOT: Not for me I'm afraid. I don't make it a habit to fraternize with students. Especially during a course of study. I take it rather seriously.

SARAH: Wow, Elliot—boundaries, decorum. What century did you drop in from?

ELLIOT: I could walk you out to your car if you like.

SARAH: No, trust me. You don't want to be seen coming out of the building with me. Your picture will be on websites within four minutes and you'll get calls the next day from kids you went to kindergarten with asking you for money. Fame is weird that way. I'll see you next week, okay?

ELLIOT: Okay.

(SARAH *smiles a little, turns and leaves.* ELLIOT *slowly starts to move about the studio, picking up props, cleaning up and getting ready to close for the day. Just as he's about to turn out the light, we hear a commotion outside the window—the sound of the paparazzi yelling, "Hey, Sarah!" "Sarah, look this way!" "Sarah! Sarah, over here!" etc and we can detect a seemingly never ending explosion of flashes as* ELLIOT *makes his way over to the window, looking down toward the craziness as the lights fade slowly to black.)*

Scene Five

(*The following Thursday*)

(*As the lights come up, we see* SARAH *standing on a riser in the corner of the studio. She's just finished presenting a monologue as* ELLIOT *sits perfectly still on a chair in front of her.*)

SARAH: That by the way—that was the uh, end of the monologue.

ELLIOT: I figured that—being that you—you know, haven't said anything for the past oh, two minutes or so.

(*Pause*)

SARAH: Right. I mean I guess I could have called "scene" —isn't that how you "legit" theater actors do it, but I didn't know if I should say that for a monologue.

ELLIOT: You should feel free to say whatever you want.

SARAH: As should you, you know, I mean rip away. Be as truthful as you need to be.

ELLIOT: Oh, I will be.

(Very long pause)

SARAH: I mean to me, it just wasn't the right piece to do, was it? I mean I'm too old for the character and I rushed through it, I know.

ELLIOT: If you'd like me to leave, maybe it would be easier if you just taught yourself.

SARAH: That's not what I meant.

ELLIOT: Do you think by being hard on yourself before I have a chance to be hard on you, that that will somehow blunt the criticism that is coming your way?

SARAH: No, no, of course not. But if I suck, just tell me.

ELLIOT: Why would I let you off that easily?

SARAH: So I was really that bad?

ELLIOT: It wasn't that you were "bad" at all—it was a perfectly adequate performance.

SARAH: "Adequate"?

ELLIOT: It did exactly what you meant it to do, Sarah. It pleased me. Every little facet of your delivery— your schlumpy apologetic posture walking up to the riser, your cutesy little self deprecating jokes before starting—charming, really, and because you're so pretty, it really kind of worked on me. So in a way Sarah, it's a good plan. Lower expectations, flirt, and underwhelm to the point of making the people who are evaluating you feel oddly superior and attracted to you at the same time. That was a performance that very well might have booked you a job. And maybe that's the point. I mean of course it is, isn't it? The point of doing work is to impress, to get a job. To win over the room as it were.

SARAH: Of course it isn't.

ELLIOT: Then the point is to make me like you, yes? Because I think the person who did that monologue— is eminently likable. A person who will never surprise me or fail or embarrass me. The person who did that monologue, is immune to failure. And I want to be around that sort of person, so I'm going to hire her. Is that how it works on that other coast?

SARAH: So I'm being taken to task for being likable?

ELLIOT: No, you're being "taken to task" for not having the balls to be anything but. You tell me you want to be a "real actress".

SARAH: I do.

ELLIOT: Well, then you might as well save your money because you already are one. You are, there is no doubt in my mind, "acting" real. I am not a camera, by the way.

SARAH: I don't understand.

ELLIOT: I'm just making an observation. It's important you know that I,—also a potential audience, the hot dog seller down on 47th street, the driver behind the wheel of your gas guzzling car…

SARAH: It's a hybrid.

ELLIOT: …of course it is. The point is, none of us is a camera. So you have to stop seducing and pleasing. And just talk. Just talk to us. Maybe even listen once in awhile. What is acting, Sarah?

SARAH: What do you mean?

ELLIOT: I'm about to let a cat out of the bag that might very well get me ex-communicated from the League of

Ne're-Do-Well Pretentious Acting Instructors. But first, just tell me—what is acting?

SARAH: Well in some ways it's impossible to define.

ELLIOT: Drank that kool-aid, did you?

SARAH: What is it then?

ELLIOT: Acting is when we make believe we are the characters we're playing.

SARAH: That's it?

ELLIOT: That's it.

SARAH: But that can't be it.

ELLIOT: No, of course it can't. It has to be more than that. There has to be a kind of "secret garden", doesn't there? Some unobtainable aspect to it. No, God forbid you remember how much fun it was to make your family laugh at the kitchen table. Even though of course, all you were doing back then was playacting. You see, Sarah—I think you're running away from that—from the fun of it, when what I think you should be doing is running toward it. I suggest you go backwards. Regress. Try to remember what it was about that time that changed your life for the better. That liberated you from something. From a silent family at dinner. Go back to the kitchen table, Sarah.

(Pause)

SARAH: Why did you stop, Elliot?

ELLIOT: Why did I stop what?

SARAH: Acting.

ELLIOT: Nice try.

SARAH: But you had a real career, you worked. You were nominated for awards—that people heard of. I mean people thought you were—

ELLIOT: —thought I was what?

SARAH: Well, that you were—brilliant. That you
were—

ELLIOT: —there are many roads to failure.

SARAH: What are you talking about "failure"? You
didn't fail.

ELLIOT: No, no, no, it's all right. Within the context
of the industry, to people who might do a little
homework, perhaps I did all right, but I have no
illusions about where I stand in the pantheon.

SARAH: I'm the failure.

ELLIOT: Say again?

SARAH: It's me. I'm the failure.

ELLIOT: Oh, please—if you're a failure—at least you
get to be one in a big beautiful house. But *real* failure,
real soul-sucking, psyche crippling failure doesn't
come knocking on the door one day and announce
itself. No, it's sort of like a vapor that gradually finds
its way under the floorboards—silently creeping up on
you until before long, you look around one day and
realize you're completely immersed in it. See what
most people don't know is—the path to real failure
is sprinkled occasionally with barely quantifiable
successes. That's how it gets you. And once it takes
hold of you, it never—ever—lets go.

SARAH: Wow, you're a drag.

ELLIOT: Oh, you should hear me at dinner parties.

SARAH: Why don't you act anymore?

ELLIOT: You're very sweet. If I could answer that
question I would. But I could tell you this: It's not
anything you think it might be. I'm not a "drunk", per
se—except, you know, occasionally, when I slip on an
adult diaper, lock myself in a closet and drink until
I pass out. And I'm not a "drug addict" —exactly—

unless of course you include the drug of control. I do like that—as you might have been able to tell.

SARAH: Just a smidge.

ELLIOT: And I wasn't awful to work with, especially when I worked alone. I've always found that with me, *other* people tend to be the problem.

SARAH: You sound like a perfect pleasure.

ELLIOT: No, I have no idea whatsoever why it didn't work out for me.

SARAH: Do you ever date your students?

ELLIOT: Excuse me?

SARAH: Oh, I mean—gosh that sounded—

ELLIOT: —it did indeed.

SARAH: I mean I didn't mean—

ELLIOT: Yes, when I mentioned I don't fraternize with students that does include my not dating them. And so in answer to your question, I do not. And even if I did—and I don't mean any offense by this—you're not exactly my type.

SARAH: Ouch.

ELLIOT: And when I say "type" —I mean gender.

SARAH: Oh. Oh, you're—

ELLIOT: —yes, they have a name for my condition now.

SARAH: No, I mean—of course you're gay.

ELLIOT: "Of course" I'm gay?

SARAH: Oh, no I didn't mean that.

ELLIOT: Well, wait, what? Did I just float through the door on gossamer wings?

SARAH: No, not at all, you seem totally straight to me.

ELLIOT: I didn't know I seemed anything.

SARAH: No, you know what I mean.

ELLIOT: Do you ever wish you could take back say—
the last thirty words you've just spoken? I bet you're
wishing that right now.

SARAH: Honestly, I didn't mean—

ELLIOT: Lets get back to your crappy monologue.

SARAH: Thank you, Elliot.

ELLIOT: For what for heavens sake?

(SARAH *starts to cry.*)

SARAH: For putting up with me. For taking me on.

ELLIOT: Oh, don't worry about it. And you won't thank
me when you get your bill. You've already wrung up,
by my estimation, about two million dollars worth of
session time today alone.

SARAH: Worth every penny.

ELLIOT: Oh, please, please, please, don't cry in acting
class. It's the cliché that makes other clichés blush.

SARAH: No, no, I'm just—I'm sorry.

ELLIOT: What I don't want to turn into here is one of
those quasi psychologist acting gurus, okay? I refuse
to be anything even approaching a Henry to your
Eliza. I don't think there's any place for that touchy
feely bullshit in a place of work. That's why I think
it's important we not get to know each other. Now
of course I don't mind the occasional "bitching about
our day" stories, but I want you to know I don't really
care about you as a person. Of course let me put that
another way. If I saw you walking into an oncoming
cab, of course I would reach out and stop you, but I
don't care about whom you date, or—your feelings
of rejection stemming from a lack of intimacy in the
household you grew up in,—any of that. I really
don't care. And I say that—however clinical it might

sound—out of respect for you as a potentially fine practitioner of our sacred craft.

SARAH: No, no, of course. I totally understand that. I don't mean to be unprofessional.

ELLIOT: Would you like to call it a day?

SARAH: *(Keeps crying)* No, no, honestly, I'm sorry. But yes, of course we should call it a day. I'm just—I'm sorry.

ELLIOT: Please don't put me in a position where I feel I have to ask you what it is you're crying about.

SARAH: No, I'm not. I am totally not asking you to ask me.

ELLIOT: But yet you persist in behaving in a way, where if I don't ask you what it is you're crying about, I risk being perceived as a callous, unfeeling ogre. And yet if I do ask what it is you're crying about, we'll be doing exactly what it was I just explained to you—I have no interest whatsoever in doing. So, as you could see, I'm somewhat between a boulder and a hard place.

SARAH: Honestly, I'm sorry, I'll just leave. I—you really, this really has been good for me, Elliot.

ELLIOT: Well, sure. Look, anytime I could send a student off into the world a blubbering wreck, I feel I've done my job.

(SARAH starts to sob again.)

ELLIOT: Oh, dear lord. Let me get you—I think I have some tissues.

SARAH: No, I've got some, thank you.

ELLIOT: I'm not going to ask, Sarah.

SARAH: That's alright, it is so not your problem.

ELLIOT: Is it a boy? Not that I'm asking, but just tell me generally—just so I could dismiss it with some sort of glib comment and send you on your way.

SARAH: No, it's not a boy. Honestly, I'm fine.

ELLIOT: You're pregnant. Not asking, so don't tell me. I don't want to hear it.

SARAH: No, I'm not pregnant.

ELLIOT: Well, whatever it is—look, let me just give you a little advice: personally, I've found that it's always better to *not* deal with your feelings—don't face them head on, don't "process" them—or any of those bull crap tactics so called modern psychology suggests we do nowadays. I never do that. I just sit on things and don't deal with them and I've never been happier. And also Sarah, take heart: if life has taught me anything, it's that no matter how bad things seem—they can— and usually do—get even worse. So chin up, young lady—something even more horrible is bound to come along and dwarf whatever this little "hiccup" is you're blubbering on about now.

SARAH: Wow, that is the worst advice I have ever gotten—ever.

ELLIOT: All right, what is it?

SARAH: I'm dying, Elliot. *(Pause)* Do you have anymore tissues? These are like—oops, sorry about the "like".

(ELLIOT *just looks at* SARAH. *She suddenly makes a bee line for the door.*)

ELLIOT: Stop!

(SARAH *stops.*)

SARAH: Please don't yell at me.

(ELLIOT *pulls up a chair for* SARAH.)

ELLIOT: Sit.

(SARAH *goes and sits in the chair. There's a considerable pause.*)

ELLIOT: So, —first off, you're not saying that to get out of being taken to task for that awful monologue, are you? Because if you are—

SARAH: Was it really that bad?

ELLIOT: It was, yes.

SARAH: So, you lied to me?

ELLIOT: Can we stay on one topic at a time, please?

SARAH: I just don't want to suck, Elliot.

ELLIOT: I didn't say you "sucked", I said your monologue did. So if we could just—if you wouldn't mind us getting back to the—other topic. What is it you mean exactly, when you say you're—you know—

SARAH: Dying?

ELLIOT: Right.

SARAH: Well, I wasn't feeling well, you know, for the longest time, and I had some suspicions about some things, and I went on the internet to try to find out what I was dying of, because I just assumed I was dying, I always assumed I was, whenever there was anything the least bit—whenever something was out of the ordinary, and the internet is the totally worst place to go because there's just so much information that no matter what symptom you Google, lists of like eighty thousand things you could be dying of come up and you just can't go that route or it will drive you absolutely crazy, so I went to a doctor I know in L A at Cedars, and he started this whole battery of tests and at first everything checked out, and I was kind of feeling really good about things and then one morning, when I was baking a batch of gluten free banana spice muffins—the phone rang. It's so funny how things

freeze in your head, but I remember looking at the
phone ringing, and it had rung about three times
before I picked it up and when I put it to my ear, it was
from *that* very instant that everything went into this
sort of slow motion dance —and I knew right away
what he was going to tell me. "Sarah?," he said, in this
super empathetic "I'm just about to tell you you're
dying voice," "Sarah, this is Dr. Jenkins. I'm afraid I
have some..." *(Pause)* And then ya know what? My
first thought was: "Wow, when I put these muffins in
the oven I didn't know I was dying, and when I took
them out—." And I thought, "Gee whiz, isn't life funny
that way?

ELLIOT: Isn't it.

SARAH: But ya know, Elliot, in some ways I was totally
relieved. For the first time in my life I wouldn't have
to worry about whether I was dying or not. Crazy, I
know, but then—I sort of am. So I hung up, walked
into my bedroom, closed the door, pulled down all
the shades and sat in the middle of my bed for sixteen
hours straight. Not crying, not spazzing out, nothing,
just sitting there, playing a black and white movie
of my entire life in my head: every crossroad, all the
wonderful things, all the bad, isolating every little
instant where I made a choice that led me down some
road, which then led me down some other road where
I would be forced to make a choice that would lead
me down some other road—all the way back to when
I could actually remember remembering. When I got
out of bed I walked into my kitchen and saw my phone
on the floor. Apparently it had vibrated so much it
vibrated itself right off the kitchen counter and onto
my brand new Italian hand crafted tile floor. And there
it was, spinning and dancing and vibrating all over
my one hundred and fourteen thousand dollar floor
and so I picked it up, checked it, and I had sixty seven

new voicemails. Twenty eight of them were from my manager, freaked that I had missed some sort of photo shoot or something, fifteen were from my agent, eleven were from my publicist, seven were from my stylist, five were from a car service and one was an automated message from the Church of Latter Day Saints. After I hung up, I ran into my room again and rifled through one of my Kate Spades and found the little piece of paper my agent had written your name and number on. I booked a flight on my way to the airport and— here I be.

(Pause)

ELLIOT: And what Sarah—if you don't mind my asking—what is the—I mean what exactly—

SARAH: —you mean what am I croaking of? I decided I would never say the word out loud. I don't want to empower it.

ELLIOT: Oh, okay. So it is—one word.

SARAH: Yup.

ELLIOT: Okay. Well, all right.

(Pause)

SARAH: Well, aren't you at least curious what letter it starts with?

ELLIOT: Oh, well, okay, "starts with a—what?" God, this is the saddest game of charades ever.

SARAH: "C." It starts with a "C".

ELLIOT: Oh. Right, okay.

SARAH: When I have to say it out loud I call it something else.

ELLIOT: Such as?

SARAH: Anything, just something silly, lighter. Lately, I've been calling it "cumquat."

ELLIOT: "Cumquat," really?

SARAH: Yes, it's a kind of fruit plant.

ELLIOT: I'm familiar, yes.

SARAH: Apparently you could also spell it with a "K", but I prefer to use the "C".

ELLIOT: Huh, well that's—why come here?

SARAH: I came to you Elliot because unlike me, you have a reputation you deserve. You have everything I don't: chops, legitimacy, experience, everything. And you call yourself a failure. I know, "poor little movie star." I know I make no discernable difference in the world whatsoever. I know where I'm at. No one will care when I die, not really anyway. I mean when some people find out, a lot of them will be sort of amused by it. My dying will only prove to them that life is fair after all. Even little Hollywood bitches draw the short straw once in awhile, so I'll be good for a few snarky comments at the water cooler or on Access Hollywood.

(*Suddenly there's a camera flash through The window of the door and an offstage voice "Hey Sarah, Sarah over here".*)

ELLIOT: What was that?

SARAH: Oh, they're sneaking up now.

ELLIOT: Hey! (*He runs out the door, chasing the unseen photographer. We hear his voice, off:*) Hey!. Get out of here! This is my—this is my property sir, and you are most certainly NOT welcome—you—you— SCOUNDREL!

(ELLIOT *comes back in, slamming the door behind him. Sarah is laughing, Elliot looks over*)

ELLIOT: What is so funny?

SARAH: Well, you—it's just—first of all, did you just call him a "scoundrel?"

ELLIOT: Can you think of a better name for someone like that?

SARAH: No, I'm sure it's— *(Continues to laugh)* I mean I just have to believe that's the first time he's ever been called a "scoundrel."

ELLIOT: Well, who is he to—just common decency, after all.

SARAH: I appreciate the gesture, Elliot. I thought it was very gallant.

ELLIOT: Look, Sarah—I don't —I don't quite know what to say. I'm afraid I'm a little stumped. I'm not very good at—situations like—

SARAH: "Situations" like what?

ELLIOT: Well, just situations in general come to think of it. Who else have you told?

SARAH: No one.

ELLIOT: "No one"?

SARAH: Only my doctor knows. I haven't told my parents. I just have to find the right time. I've started treatments, uptown, but they made clear to me what the odds are. I didn't mean to lay all of this on you, Elliot.

ELLIOT: Don't be silly.

SARAH: There is one role out there, though. One role I'd really like the sink my teeth into before I, you know—

ELLIOT: Oh, no.

SARAH: No, I know, I know this class isn't about getting a job. But this is for a meaningful film—not like the one on the side of the bus. And it's British, the film and the writer, so even if it ends up sucking, most people will just hear those accents and assume it's brilliant anyway.

ELLIOT: Dear lord.

SARAH: It's the role of this amazing daughter, —and how she does and doesn't get along with her mother. It's about her growing up—and she's funny and has more than just one dimension and there's no nudity in it or gross language, and some of the speeches even have more than three sentences in them.

ELLIOT: No kidding.

SARAH: No, they're almost monologues. And you know how good I am at those, Elliot. Anyway, I brought it up to my agent, and he told me to forget it. He said I should take the offer on the space movie sequel, buy an island and pay someone to suck my toes.

ELLIOT: I don't know how agents get the reputations they have.

SARAH: I really want this, Elliot. I really think I could bring something to it.

ELLIOT: This isn't how I work.

SARAH: And I promise not to use the fact that I'm dying in order to gain your sympathy. That is of course, unless I absolutely have to. *(She smiles.)*

ELLIOT: I must say I don't like the way you're talking.

SARAH: What do you mean, did I just say "like" again?

ELLIOT: No, I mean the way you're talking about your—situation. As though it's already a foregone conclusion, as though there's no hope at all.

SARAH: I know—you know about losing someone, Elliot.

(ELLIOT looks at SARAH.)

SARAH: Anyway, I better go. I have seventy five interviews to do for the crappy space movie tomorrow, one right after another. And in all of them it's important I appear chipper, supportive of the movie and most of all—not dying. (*She walks over to him, kisses him on the cheek.*) See you next week.

(SARAH *walks out.* ELLIOT *stands still as the lights fade to black*)

Scene Six

(*The following Thursday*)

(SARAH *walks excitedly into the studio, holds something up for* ELLIOT *to see.*)

SARAH: Look what I got!

ELLIOT: Pray tell.

SARAH: They call it a "Metro card". It's for the subway.

ELLIOT: Really?

SARAH: I had no idea the worlds this little card would open up for me. Did you know the subway is the fastest mode of travel on the island of Manhattan, and that people from all different socio-economic strata ride on it?

ELLIOT: Well aren't you a veritable fountain of information today.

SARAH: Well here's the thing: They couldn't find me. They couldn't keep up with me.

ELLIOT: Who are you talking about?

SARAH: The creeps with the cameras. I hopped on "the number 6"— ever heard of it?

ELLIOT: I believe I have heard it referenced a time or two.

SARAH: —well, I jumped on it, and for the life of them, they couldn't find me. I blended right in with the sea of humanity. It was amazing, Elliot—it was wonderful.

And some people recognized me and seemed to not care at all, and some people kind of recognized me and just sort of nodded—almost sweetly, as if to say "I see you. I recognize you. I will however, not bother you." Miraculous.

ELLIOT: It's almost as though you were in the real world.

SARAH: It was weird. And from block to block in this city, it's like it takes on different looks, different feels.

ELLIOT: Yes, they call them "neighborhoods".

SARAH: Well, it's just been some time since I—

ELLIOT: What?

SARAH: Well, its embarrassing, I know—but its been the longest time since I've really been around people. I mean really—among them.

ELLIOT: It'll help, ya know?

SARAH: What will?

ELLIOT: Well, breezing around from one place to the other in the backs of cars, hotels, gated homes, press junkets, private jets—people to steer you this way and that, its dreamy, I'm sure, and in many ways must be kind of a delicious life—and I mean that, I'm not being condescending. It is a dream, and there's nothing wrong with it. But it can separate you from the well that you will need to draw from—to inform your best work. The scary looking guy outside the McDonalds on Eight Avenue who keeps trying to pass you that flyer, the pissed off girl on her lunch hour who breaks her heel in front of you, and has to hobble over to the fire hydrant while simultaneously breaking up with her boyfriend on her cell phone—all these little moments hold secrets. To how people behave. The world they live in. And it's your job to unlock those secrets and find a way to inform whatever character it is you're playing. Your busting out of the gilded cage, Sarah—that's probably the best education you'll get while you're here. Not whatever pearls of wisdom I might throw your way.

SARAH: I told them.

ELLIOT: "Them" being?

SARAH: My mom and dad.

ELLIOT: Ah. Not a phone call I'd wish on any parent.

SARAH: They were amazing Elliot. My mom was making reservations to fly here while my father was trying to keep me from hearing him cry on the phone. He kept saying he had a cold—so sweet.

ELLIOT: I'm very glad to hear that. *(Beat)* —By the by I took a read of the script for that Brit flick you sent me. What's it called again? *(He finds the script, reads off it.)* "This Summers Eve." Amazing what the English can get away with.

SARAH: Isn't she a gorgeous character?

ELLIOT: She is. Smart, engaged.

SARAH: And she wins in every way.

ELLIOT: Wins the man, you mean?

SARAH: No, the fight. She wins herself back in the end, not just the man.

ELLIOT: In some ways it made me recall *Hamlet*, page twenty four especially, when Eloise confronts her mother—do you have yours?

(SARAH takes out her copy of the screenplay.)

SARAH: Got it.

ELLIOT: So first answer me this: Why doesn't Hamlet just ask Claudius whether he killed his father or not?

SARAH: Because then it would be a very short play.

ELLIOT: That's true, but there's another reason as well. One having more to do with human nature. Which, I hasten to remind you—is something one's performance is supposed to in some way reflect.

SARAH: But in this scene, she's just trying to talk to her mother.

ELLIOT: All I'm doing is trying to make connections where I can. Especially when dealing in this—genre, or form or whatever you want to call it.

SARAH: Is "genre" pretentious-speak for "movie"?

ELLIOT: Of course not.

SARAH: Well then why can't you just call this what it is? It's a movie.

ELLIOT: I'm simply trying to find connective tissue. Why doesn't Hamlet ask the king right off?

SARAH: Because it isn't what people do.

ELLIOT: Exactly. If I want to express something awkward or awful to someone, the first thing I do is try to figure out a way not to. So instead I stand in a certain way, or avoid making eye contact or if I do look at someone, there's a way to do it so as to conceal what my true intent actually is. Most people don't profess their love. Most people don't tell the people they hate—that they hate them. Most of us just drift through life coming only so close to telling people how we actually feel about them. Most people behave Sarah, they don't express—they behave. And of course the best writers know that. And Shakespeare, you'll forgive me, I think if he keeps it up—just might have a real future that way.

SARAH: So I forget the words.

ELLIOT: No, you memorize them, yes—what you "forget" is your tendency to imbue them with pre-conceived notions of so called "meaning" and "intent." And in this scene in particular, in the screenplay, when Eloise walks into a room wanting to say something to her mother, and in her heart of hearts knows that it could go one of two ways: either her mother is going to be receptive to her, and there's a chance they could reconcile after five years—or, as she's done for that entire time or longer, her mother could dash her heart against the rocks and destroy what's left of her already fragile psyche. But in the end, there's still only one way—from an actor's standpoint, to even begin approaching a scene like this.

SARAH: And that is—

ELLIOT: —to walk into the room. *(Pause)* You see that's how the scene begins. It says it right here, "Eloise walks into the room."

SARAH: And so what happens after that—depends—

ELLIOT: —not on what you've rehearsed.

SARAH: Okay.

ELLIOT: Or God forbid studied.

SARAH: Okay.

ELLIOT: But only on what happens *after*—

SARAH: —after I've—

ELLIOT: —no, not you—

SARAH: —after Eloise—

ELLIOT: —right—

SARAH: —has walked into the room.

ELLIOT: By George I think she's got it! *(Singing a la* My Fair Lady*)* —"By George I think she's got it, she's got it, she's got it, By George I think—"

(SARAH *playfully hits* ELLIOT.)

SARAH: Shut up, Elliot. Stop making fun of me.

ELLIOT: I don't mean to, honestly. It's just—well, it's just so much damn fun.

(*Pause*)

SARAH: But it's frightening, isn't it? Not knowing. I mean both for the character and me.

ELLIOT: Well, see it's funny how that tends to coincide, isn't it?

SARAH: So then the truth is it's okay to *not* know, and when I walk through a door—in real life, and in the movie, I'm not acting at all. You see I always assumed it was knowing. Knowing, knowing, knowing, knowing. Knowing everything, preparation. Driving it deep into my skull.

ELLIOT: It absolutely *is* preparation, and we do "prepare"—but only to the point where we feel confident enough to forget everything we've prepared for. It's a slippery slope, but a thrilling one. Look, when I walk through a door, I never know what's going to be on the other side. I could have an idea, a pre-conceived notion maybe, but the truth is —I never really know.

SARAH: And that's okay. It's okay to not know. Even to be scared of what might come next.

ELLIOT: "Okay"? "Okay"?, it's GREAT! Scared is great. Try to be scared as much as you can be—especially in performance.

SARAH: But why didn't I know any of this?

ELLIOT: Oh, well see if you had, you might be making eight instead of your measly seven million dollars a picture.

SARAH: No but seriously, Elliot, this is all new to me.

ELLIOT: It is to me as well, Sarah. Every day is. This is something you learn everyday and practice everyday. Allow yourself to be spontaneous. Allow yourself not to know.

SARAH: It's such a joke anyway. I mean even if I could somehow fudge my way past a physical, it's not like I have a chance of getting this part. My agent says I'm an idiot for even trying. Plus I'm putting myself on tape—offering to fly myself out. Already I "reek of desperation" he says.

ELLIOT: Well, maybe—or perhaps you "reek" of passion. You never know how they're going to perceive you.

SARAH: But then how would you know? It's been years since you've auditioned, hasn't it?

ELLIOT: I don't remember.

SARAH: Oh, come on, I'm not getting personal.

ELLIOT: You're not a horrible actor, but your real skill is coercing people into talking about things they don't want to talk about.

SARAH: You mean I'm a nudge.

ELLIOT: As good a word as any.

SARAH: Come on, horrible audition story, just one.

ELLIOT: Audition stories bore me.

SARAH: Oh come on, they do not. Just one, all I'm asking.

ELLIOT: Well, it really wasn't so much an audition as it was a—travesty.

SARAH: I knew I'd get you. Come on, spill the beans.

ELLIOT: Well it's funny you should mention "beans."

SARAH: Why?

ELLIOT: I was reading for *Comedy of Errors*. If you're interested at all, Errors is the play among Shakespeare's that lends itself the most to fart jokes. It tends to be the main reason why most people do it in fact.

SARAH: Oh no.

ELLIOT: Oh, yes. And so there I stood, all of seventeen—in front of the artistic director of the summer theatre and his many minions—reciting the following from the *Comedy of Errors*— "A man may break a word with you, Sir, and words are but wind—". I suddenly stop, feel that inescapable inevitability, a rumbling in my stomach, then— elongated fart. Silence in the room. The artistic director just looks at me. Everyone agrees to say nothing, to act as though it didn't happen. On I go. "Ay, and break it in your face"—I let go of a second one, clipped. A suppressed chuckle is heard from the stage manager. I forge ahead. "So he break it not behind." Third and final sustained—and when I say "sustained" —I mean, sustaaaaaaaaaained fart. At which point, the entire room explodes in laughter. I mumble something about having a stomach flu—then I ever so courteously bow—turn on my heels, and walk out the door without once looking back.

SARAH: Did you get the job?

ELLIOT: Shockingly, no.

SARAH: Oh my God, that is the worst. You should have laughed with them.

ELLIOT: Like I said, I was seventeen, and had less of a sense of humor than then I have now—if you can believe it. You know it's funny we're even talking about auditions.

SARAH: Why is that?

ELLIOT: I got a call from my agent yesterday.

SARAH: Why is that so strange?

ELLIOT: Well, mostly because he hasn't called me in seven years. When he said he was my "agent", I assumed it had something to do with my life insurance policy.

SARAH: What did he want?

ELLIOT: Apparently *Present Laughter* is coming up at the Kennedy Center and, well—

SARAH: "Well," what?

ELLIOT: Well, it seems the director is "interested" in me for it.

SARAH: Elliot, that's wonderful!

ELLIOT: It was quite the surprise.

SARAH: When would you start?

ELLIOT: Oh, even if I were to get it, I don't know if I'm up to it frankly. I mean I'm a little rusty, to be sure. Besides, I've got my work cut out for me with you, haven't I?

SARAH: Oh, please, Elliot, I'll be fine. Stewart is an amazing, director. He'll hold your hand if he has to.

(Pause)

ELLIOT: Funny, I don't remember mentioning who was directing it.

SARAH: Didn't you?

ELLIOT: No, in fact I'm sure I didn't.

SARAH: Well, it's—it's Stewart Kimbell, isn't it?

ELLIOT: Yes, indeed it is. And how would you have known that?

(SARAH just stares back at ELLIOT.)

ELLIOT: Well, I think we can both surmise how you would know that. You rang him up with that pretty little movie star finger of yours, didn't you? And me, making a fool of myself— "Oh, did I mention my agent called me" —what a ridiculous idiot, I am. What a stupid naïve buffoon. No doubt you regaled your director friend with the piteous tale of your broken down old acting teacher, eh?

SARAH: Elliot stop. So I made a call. Stewart is someone I worked with when I was a teenager on a mini-series. He's a wonderful man. All I did was remind him of how brilliant you were. So I made a call. Can you imagine that? Someone in show business calling on behalf of someone else? Oh, what a travesty! Did I violate some kind of "ideal of purity"—some kind of warped code of theatrical ethics—well so what, Elliot!? All you are is scared. You're just scared to get on the stage again.

ELLIOT: Do you not remember what I said about our getting to know each other too well?

SARAH: Elliot, what happened during that play in New Haven is pretty well documented.

ELLIOT: What do you know about that?

SARAH: All anyone has to do is Google, Elliot. The point is you lost someone. You lost someone very close to you, that you loved—Derrick Lawson, right? The designer?

ELLIOT: —careful—

SARAH: And when you were on stage that night—you "saw something" you said.

ELLIOT: That's enough.

SARAH: And whose to say you didn't? You stopped the play, you smashed the set and you screamed, you screamed to hundreds of people that you saw a ghost.

ELLIOT: I never said it was a ghost, it was a "vision, I said.

SARAH: Well whatever it was, maybe he was visiting you, trying to get something across to you. Or maybe you felt guilty, because some people said you abandoned him—or—

ELLIOT: Who said that?

SARAH: It was a scary time, Elliot, a new disease, nobody knew…

(ELLIOT *explodes.*)

ELLIOT: —how DARE you!

SARAH: What?

ELLIOT: Do you not have *any* respect, any common decency? Do you think this is some kind of reality show? Do you ever think—even just *think*, that some things—should not be spoken of? Not be aired, not be exploited or consumed? My god woman, you didn't even have the decency to keep the fact that you are *dying* from me.

SARAH: Elliot—

ELLIOT: Well think about it. What business is that of mine? What business was it ever of mine?

SARAH: It's none. It's none of your business, you're right, and this is none of mine, but—Elliot, Elliot, I'm sorry—I—

ELLIOT: —I no longer feel under any obligation to stand here week after week and listen to your stupid, vapid, self-involved drivel. I don't need to be put through a ringer by someone who has little or no —even rudimentary understanding of what the craft, what the art of acting—even potentially consists of. You are an embarrassment. You and your crass, meaningless and hollow "notoriety" represents nothing but

confirmation that our society is in its final throes.
You are known by millions of people—and yet you
consist of nothing. You are little more than a concocted
vapor that stands as a mockery to the thousands and
thousands of trained, respectful actors who tread
the boards in total obscurity—night after night—
Shakespeare in basements, Chekhov in attics and how
dare YOU—speak to me—about anything. GET OUT!

SARAH: Elliot, please—

ELLIOT: OUT!

(SARAH *stands frozen, then slowly starts to collect her*
things. She picks up her purse and slowly walks toward the
door as ELLIOT *looks away. She stops, just before she gets to*
the door. Looks toward him. Seems as though she might say
something, then turns and walks out. He stands alone as the
lights fade slowly to black.)

Scene Seven

(*A few days later*)

(ELLIOT *walks in the studio, taking off his hat and*
addressing the audience as though it were his class.)

ELLIOT: No, no, don't bother taking out your little
notebooks—I'm canceling class—and class in general
for the rest of the year. And for the foreseeable future,
assuming there even is one. I'm just not—well, I
suppose I could make up some excuse, but—people
in my line of work—we lie to you for a living anyway,
so what's the point? We stand up here week after
week and prattle on as if we know what we're talking
about—or that what we do makes a difference. I wish
I could tell you that that were the case. The truth is
of course, it isn't. Run. (*Pause*) Did you not hear me?
I said run! If you ever hope to have any chance at all,
each and every fresh faced one of you needs to turn

tail and run from people like me—now! If you want
to learn something, buy a book. The irony of course
being—that I act as if I know what acting is. The truth
is I have no idea. All it is, is mirrors—slight of hand,
a well timed distraction, fun and games and smoke
up your ass. Do spread the word, will you? Elliot's a
bloody nutcase—a certifiable crackpot—tell everyone
you know that I stood right here—right in front of you
—and I warned you: Do NOT ignore the man behind
the curtain. In fact, should you get the chance—rip
his throat out and bash his skull in for good measure.
Because what is this anyway? Really? What is this? A
parlor game—that's all it is really. A parlor game —
with pretensions. Want my respect? Throw yourself
down an abyss while whistling a happy little tune—hit
bottom, then drop me a line, because then—and only
then, will we have something to talk about. Until that
time, suckers, don't let the truth hit you on the way
out—and turn off the lights, will you?

(ELLIOT *puts his hat back on, smiles toward his students,
then turns and walks out the door. Lights bump to black.*)

Scene Eight

(*Almost a year later*)

(*As the lights come up, we see* SARAH *standing near the
window, looking down toward the street. She is hardly
recognizable. She's exhausted looking and wearing a kerchief
on her head, covered by a bright, self consciously cheery hat.
She is leaning on a bright red cane. After a moment,* ELLIOT
*enters. He stops short, can't believe he sees her. She turns
toward him. After a pause:*)

ELLIOT: Ten months, four days, sixteen hours—and
about forty—what? (*Looks at his watch*) seven?—

seconds—since you walked out this door—not that I'm counting.

SARAH: Hello, Elliot.

ELLIOT: I tried calling that number—

SARAH: —I changed it.

ELLIOT: And your agent. I wrote time and time—

SARAH: —I don't have an agent anymore, Elliot. By the way is it me or is this place even grosser than usual?

ELLIOT: It hasn't been used much lately.

SARAH: Yeah, I heard about the little "pep talk" you gave awhile back.

ELLIOT: Yes, it's been quite the interesting year. (Pause) Sarah, before we say anything else—I wanted to—I can't even begin to tell you how—

SARAH: —oh, Elliot, please no sing song voice. Everyone talks that way to me now. I call it "cancer voice".

ELLIOT: You said the word.

SARAH: What? Oh, yeah I started a few months ago. Would you believe I started to feel sorry for it? Yes, that's right—I do. I feel sorry for cancer. Such an un-cool way to die nowadays. Can't do movies about cancer—too familiar. Too pedestrian and easy. Aneurysms however? That would be fine. Rickets, scurvy, sure, —anything a pirate might die of, fine, but cancer? Not so much I'm afraid.

ELLIOT: I'm so relieved to see you're still insane. And I like the color of your cane.

SARAH: Do you really? I do too. I thought it was kind of Christmassy.

ELLIOT: When you told me—when you confided in me,—you see I lost Derrick in much the same way. A different, much cooler disease of course, then cancer —

SARAH: —you don't have to say anything.

ELLIOT: Oh, I do.

SARAH: You don't owe me a thing. I'm the one who should apologize to you.

ELLIOT: I wasn't there for him—when he needed me most. Don't mistake me—I was in the room, but I wasn't there.

SARAH: Well, someone you loved was dying—right in front of you—

ELLIOT: —oh, no, no, thank you for your generous assumption, but no—I was just a coward. *(Pause)* Oh, I saw that movie by the way. The British one. They were wrong not to cast you.

SARAH: I thought the so called star they cast— "whatshername" —did a good job.

ELLIOT: Sure, "whatshername" was fine—in a tinny, superficial, remedial kind of "struggling to find even the remotest handle on the character" sort of way. But no, other than that I thought she was fine.

ELLIOT: I have a confession to make to you.

SARAH: No kidding. Is it juicy?

ELLIOT: Sort of I suppose.

SARAH: Well spill it.

ELLIOT: Wait, sit down for goodness sakes.

(ELLIOT helps SARAH into a chair.)

SARAH: Thank you.

ELLIOT: All right, well—I don't want to seem like what you might call a "stalker," or an obsessed fan or anything like that. But, a few weeks after we last saw each other, I started watching your movies.

SARAH: *My* movies?

ELLIOT: Yes, shocking I know. And yes, while some of them tried to be more—most of them in fact were little more than dumb, simplistic brain candy. I could see why they made so much money. Still, that said—

SARAH: Yes?

ELLIOT: You, Sarah—are a wonderful actress.

(Pause)

SARAH: Shut up, Elliot.

ELLIOT: No, no, no, you must not dismiss this out of hand.

SARAH: You wouldn't say that if I still had hair.

ELLIOT: No, no, that is NOT true. You are still in my workspace here, so you shut up Sarah and when you hear someone say something nice to you, don't immediately dismiss it because you still have lingering issues with daddykins. I don't hand out compliments like candy and I don't have to say this and I don't give a crap whether in your heart you believe it or not. I'm simply saying this: The young woman I saw awash in those cinematic confections—the young woman I saw working in them had moments...and not just a few of them, that convinced me she had real—not transient, not lucky and fleeting—but *real* talent. You are a wonderful actress, Sarah. You never needed me. It was already there. There is a reason people like seeing you up on that screen.

(Pause. SARAH tries to hide the fact that she's crying.)

ELLIOT: Oh dear, I've done it again. Haven't I?

SARAH: Well, Elliot, you've never been nice to me before.

ELLIOT: Well for goodness sakes don't tell anyone. I don't want to ruin my reputation.

SARAH: You're a wonderful teacher. Please don't quit.

ELLIOT: Well, I will uh—I will certainly take that under advisement.

SARAH: Marry me Elliot.

ELLIOT: Excuse me?

SARAH: Marry me. It would make things easier.

ELLIOT: "Easier?"

SARAH: I want to leave you something. And if we're married, it'll just make things easier for you, tax wise.

ELLIOT: No.

SARAH: Oh come on, Elliot—to be frank with you—the way you dress embarrasses me. And this filthy studio, I mean, I know you have to keep up your artistic "cred" and all that, but my God, would it kill you to have someone mop up in here once in awhile?

ELLIOT: Even when you insult me I find you impossibly adorable.

SARAH: So what do you say?

ELLIOT: Leave it to your parents.

SARAH: My parents are fine, Elliot.

ELLIOT: Then give it to someone who really needs it.

SARAH: Elliot—

ELLIOT: Leave it to a charity, Sarah. Not a charity case.

(Pause)

SARAH: All right, but I will leave you something, mark my words. *(Pause, then directly at him)* You taught me to walk through doors, Elliot. And that's what I'm about to do, aren't I?

(ELLIOT *just looks at* SARAH, *then turns away.*)

SARAH: Sorry I didn't mean to—don't worry, I know how you are about emotional interactions. Besides, who's to say I'm dying anyway, right? What the hell do doctors know?

(ELLIOT *turns around quickly.*)

ELLIOT: Well, see that's my point exactly. I think it's about time you look reality straight in the face, Sarah, and then turn the other way. Completely deny it with all the strength you have in the world.

SARAH: I will, I promise.

ELLIOT: What do you say we get to work again? Get back on the old horse? Next week sometime?

SARAH: I would love that.

ELLIOT: And be warned, I'm going to work you so hard you won't have time to die. When do you want to start again? (*He moves to his appointment book.*)

SARAH: Next Thursday at four?

ELLIOT: Perfect. And I'm not going to treat you with kid gloves this time. I want you to memorize three, no, four new monologues for next week's class. I've been way too easy on you when it comes to material. And for goodness sakes, no more *Our Town* monologues please, try a couple Shakespeares.

SARAH: I will.

ELLIOT: Alright, next Thursday at four then?

SARAH: Next Thursday at four. See you then.

ELLIOT: Right, see you then.

(SARAH *starts to slowly get up, which is difficult for her.* ELLIOT *makes a point of turning away, not wanting her to feel self conscious. Just as she's about to exit, he calls out to her*)

ELLIOT: Sarah.

(ELLIOT *quickly moves across the studio and takes* SARAH *in his arms. They hold each other tightly as the lights fade slowly to black.*)

Epilogue

(Two months later)

(As the lights come up, we see ELLIOT *entering the studio and walking right in front of the audience as though they were a new class of students.)*

ELLIOT: First off, if anyone shows up from this point on, he or she is late, and will not be admitted until next week's class so boo bloody hoo for them. Oh, and please if you would be so kind, take those computer poddie MP3 Walkman thingies or whatever you call them out of your ears. I think if you're going to take a class, you might as well be able to hear the teacher, don't you? All right, did you do as instructed? Did you write your little questions down? *(He sees the hat).* Oh, goody—let us have a look then, shall we? *(He picks up the hat. It's filled with white slips of folded paper.)* All right, first question: *(He unfolds paper, reads aloud)* "Are you always such an asshole?" In fact, I am. Next! *(He throws the paper away, unfolds another one—reads aloud)* "Were you on that cop show last night?" Yes, indeed I was. You should know that your teacher is both an actor and an acting teacher. This sometimes necessitates my being what someone might call—a "whore". Which means with any luck, you'll be seeing me on a Doritos commercial during the super bowl next January. Also, you should know I'm engaged to play *King Lear*—next fall in fact, at the Wallington Playhouse in beautiful downtown Wallington, New Jersey. Do try to contain your envy. Next! *(He throws away that piece of paper, unfolds another, reading aloud:)* "The red cane. Is it an affectation or do you really need it?

(ELLIOT turns, walks to the back of the studio and picks up SARAH's red cane, which up to this point in this scene has been hidden from view. He twirls it, turning to the class:)

ELLIOT: Is it an affectation? I suppose it most certainly is. Do I "need" it? *(Pause, looks directly at the class)* More than you will ever know. All right, then—get off your lazy butts and let's start with a little thing I like to call "breathing," shall we? And... Breathe! Breathe! Breathe!

(ELLIOT comes to a stop, holding SARAH's cane up—smiling toward it—as the lights begin to fade slowly—and he continues:)

ELLIOT: "Breathe!"

(As the light fade to black.)

END OF PLAY

www.ingramcontent.com/pod-product-compliance
Lightning Source LLC
Chambersburg PA
CBHW070030110426
42741CB00035B/2706